Pepper

Pepper

Valerie Aikman-Smith

photography by Erin Kunkel

More than 45
recipes using the
'king of spices',
from the aromatic
to the fiery

RYLAND PETERS & SMALL
LONDON • NEW YORK

First published in 2016 by
Ryland Peters & Small
20–21 Jockey's Fields,
London WC1R 4BW
and
341 E 116th St,
New York NY 10029
www.rylandpeters.com

10 9 8 7 6 5 4 3 2 1

Text © Valerie Aikman-Smith
2016
Design and photographs
© Ryland Peters & Small 2016

ISBN: 978-1-84975-710-2

Printed and bound in China

A CIP record for this book
is available from the
British Library.

US library of congress
cataloging-in-publication
date has been applied for.

Senior Designer Megan Smith
Editor Gillian Haslam
Commissioning Editor Stephanie Milner
Head of Production Patricia Harrington
Art Director Leslie Harrington
Editorial Director Julia Charles
Publisher Cindy Richards
Food and Prop Styling Valerie Aikman-Smith

Contents

Introduction

The mighty little peppercorn – once known as the 'king of spices' – is a mainstay in any cook's kitchen. Each time I pick up my peppermill, I am immediately transported to the faraway exotic lands this tiny, robust, jewel-like spice comes from, and reminded of its importance throughout history. Alongside salt and other spices, historically pepper played a powerful role in shaping trade routes around the world and creating wealth for the spice merchants. It's also a prominent feature in Indian Ayurvedic medicine and is used to help relieve many conditions, including colds and coughs – Hippocrates mixed pepper with other spices to treat fevers and the Ancient Romans believed it an antidote to poison.

Small and colourful, peppercorns are packed with an arsenal of flavours, which range from fiery and spicy to earthy, and even include bright citrus tones. The berries grow in clusters on a tropical vine (*Piper nigrum*) and are picked and dried in the sun. Originating in India, pepper is now cultivated on a commercial scale in Vietnam, Brazil, Indonesia, China and Malaysia.

There is a wide variety of pepper to choose from, depending on whether you are baking, seasoning marinades and rubs, or flavouring preserves. Use brightly coloured peppercorns to cure and pickle. Stir freshly ground white pepper into a creamy, silky Béchamel sauce and drizzle over pan-roasted fish. Add a little heat to curries and stir fries by using crushed Szechuan peppercorns. Season thick-cut steaks with robust Tellicherry pepper and make classic French sauces with briny green peppercorns. Mix with fresh spices and place in your peppermill to grind as a finishing touch over pastas, soups and salads. If you are lucky, you may to be able to locate fresh peppercorns and they can be stirred into slow-cooked stews and curries.

Buy peppercorns from the freshest source and in small quantities, as they tend to lose their punch after about six months. Specialist spice shops or online stores are the best place, as in supermarkets they may lose their flavour by sitting on the shelves for too long. Look out for Fairtrade labels and buy organic wherever possible. Make sure the peppercorns have a good colour and a strong aroma. Buy them whole so that you can crack or grind them in a peppermill or pestle and mortar. Store in airtight containers and place in a cool, dark cupboard before filling up your peppermill.

Pepper directory

1 Rainbow peppercorns
A mix of green, red, white and black peppercorns, which gives a lively look to any food when freshly ground.

2 Green peppercorns
Harvested in the Mysore region in southern India, these come from the same plant as black peppercorns and are picked unripe. They are an earthy green colour and have a wonderful fresh, bright flavour.

3 Sansho peppercorns
Harvested in Kochi, Japan and similar to Szechuan peppercorns with their heat and tingly, numbing effect. These are the unripe fruit from the ash tree and are wonderfully fiery, with a divine citrus flavour.

4 & 5 Brined peppercorns
Green peppercorns brined in salt water have a more intense taste than dried peppercorns. They give dishes a powerful, earthy heat that works well in sauces and pâtés. They are used extensively in Asian cooking in soups.

6 Tellicherry peppercorns
Left to mature for longer on the vine, these have a deep, dark, bold flavour and are a little larger than regular peppercorns. Hailing from the Malabar coast of south-west India, they are picked when red, then left to dry and turn black in the sun.

7 Pink peppercorns
These gorgeous, bright pink, jewel-like peppercorns originally came from the French island of Réunion in the Indian Ocean. Today they are mostly grown in Brazil. Although not a true peppercorn, they have similar traits with a sweet taste and a little heat.

8 Lampong black peppercorns
Cultivated in Indonesia, these peppercorns are not allowed to stay on the vine for long and are picked as soon as they ripen, which yields a sweet, woody and hot flavour. They work well with all types of food, but especially with Asian cuisine.

9 Smoked peppercorns
These black peppercorns have been slowly smoked in flavours such as hickory, mesquite and bourbon. There are many artisanal smoking recipes to choose from. The smoky, dark, robust flavours work really well in rubs, marinades and sauces.

10 Szechuan peppercorns
These are not truly peppercorns. They are native to Szechuan province in China and are the outer shell of the fruit from an aromatic shrub in the rue family. They have a jewel-like tone of dark red and pale green, and have a wonderful fiery numbing taste that then gives way to sweetness.

11 White peppercorns
These come from Sarawak in Borneo where they are grown on small farms. Picked black and ripe, they are then soaked in water to soften and remove the shell. They have a wonderful musky aroma and are hotter than most black peppercorns. They are especially good for seasoning white sauces and cheese dishes.

12 Long pepper
These grow on a luscious green, shiny, flowering vine with small black pepper spikes. Harvested in India and Indonesia, it is known for its healing remedies. It has a fruity aroma, which is much hotter than black pepper, with a good heat that lingers.

13 Malabar peppercorns
Harvested in the state of Kerala on India's Malabar coast, they are picked and dried in the sun where they turn black. They have a unique sharp heat with a robust, sweet earthiness.

Small bites

Tempura green beans dusted with Hachimi Togarashi is a match made in heaven.

Haricots verts tempura

200 g/1½ cups rice flour
½ teaspoon ground Hachimi Togarashi peppermill mix (page 53), plus extra for dusting
½ teaspoon sea salt
1 egg
350 ml/1¼ cups soda water/club soda
vegetable oil, for frying
450 g/1 lb. haricots verts, trimmed

SERVES 4

Put all the ingredients except the oil and haricots verts in a blender and process for about 30 seconds until mixed, then pour into a shallow bowl.

Pour enough oil to come halfway up a wide medium-sized saucepan, then set over a medium–high heat until the oil starts to simmer.

Working in batches, dip the beans in the batter and deep fry for 3–4 minutes until golden and cooked. Transfer to a wire rack to drain, dust with Hachimi Togarashi and serve.

Spicy and crunchy, you won't be able to stop eating these snack beans.

North African roasted chickpeas

1 tablespoon harissa paste
1 tablespoon extra virgin olive oil
1 teaspoon cracked smoked peppercorns
1 teaspoon ground coriander
1 teaspoon ground cumin
1 teaspoon sea salt
2 x 400-g/14-oz. cans of chickpeas, drained and rinsed

SERVE AS A SNACK

Preheat the oven to 200°C (400°F) Gas 6.

In a bowl whisk together the harissa, oil, pepper, coriander, cumin and salt until combined. Add the chickpeas and toss to coat.

Spread the chickpeas out in an even layer on a baking sheet and roast in the preheated oven for 30 minutes. Shake the pan halfway through cooking. Remove from the oven and cool before serving. Store in an airtight container for up to 1 week.

Sold as street food in China, these eggs make a fun addition to a Chinese feast.

'Street hawker' tea eggs

6 eggs, hard-boiled/hard-cooked
1 black tea bag
4 star anise
1 teaspoon five-spice powder
2 teaspoons cracked Szechuan pepper
1 cinnamon stick
120 ml/½ cup soy sauce
sea salt and ground Chinese Five-spice peppermill mix (page 53), to serve

MAKES 6

Gently roll the eggs on a work surface to crack the eggshells all over.

Put the remaining ingredients except those to serve into a pan and pour over 475 ml/2 cups of water. Bring to the boil over a high heat, then reduce to a simmer and cook for 5 minutes.

Remove from the heat and add the eggs to the saucepan. Allow the liquid to cool, then refrigerate overnight.

Remove the eggs from the liquid and peel. Cut in half and sprinkle with salt and some Chinese Five-spice mix.

There's a taste of the souk in this pepper crust with the glorious delicate perfume of rose petals.

Homemade ricotta cheese in a pepper crust

950 ml/4 cups whole milk
120 ml/½ cup double/heavy cream
1 teaspoon coarse sea salt
1½ tablespoons organic distilled white wine vinegar
2 tablespoons ground Moroccan Rose Petal peppermill mix (page 53)

MAKES ABOUT 450 G/2 CUPS

Put the milk, cream and salt in a large pan and bring to the boil. Remove from the heat and add the vinegar. Stir, then cover and set aside to cool.

Line a sieve/strainer with cheesecloth/muslin and place over a large bowl. Strain the mixture into the bowl. Cover and refrigerate overnight.

Roll the cheese up tightly in a piece of clingfilm/plastic wrap. Unwrap and roll in the Moroccan Rose Petal peppermill mix to serve.

Inspired by Californian wine country, these grapes are a wonderful addition to a cheeseboard or salad.

Vine-roasted grapes

450 g/1 lb. seedless red grapes on the vine
1 tablespoon extra virgin olive oil
2 teaspoons fennel pollen or ground fennel
1 teaspoon cracked Tellicherry black peppercorns
1 teaspoon coarse sea salt
6 sprigs of fresh thyme

MAKES 450 G/1 LB.

Preheat the oven to 190°C (375°F) Gas 5.

Put the grapes in a large ovenproof dish. Drizzle with the oil, then sprinkle with the fennel, pepper and salt. Gently turn the grapes to coat with mixture. Place the sprigs of thyme on and around the grapes. Roast in the preheated oven for 45 minutes, turning halfway through.

The grapes are best served at room temperature.

Serve this briny, peppery honey drizzled over cheese or grilled meats or whisked into vinaigrette. Try stirring it into a cocktail for an unusual twist.

Pepper-infused honey

2 strings of brined green peppercorns (if you can't buy strings of peppercorns, use 2 tablespoons instead)
560 g/2 cups organic wildflower honey

MAKES 560 G/2 CUPS

Place the peppercorns in a sterilized jar with a tightly fitting lid. Pour in the honey and screw on the lid. Leave to infuse for 1 week before using. The longer you leave the honey, the more intense the taste.

A wonderful Scottish classic, oatcakes are lovely to serve with cheese, pâté and spreads. You can cut the dough into strips, triangles or squares, or use cookie cutters.

Rainbow pepper oatcakes

235 g/2½ cups rolled oats
2 teaspoons cracked rainbow peppercorns
2 teaspoons coarse sea salt
½ teaspoon bicarbonate of soda/baking soda
2 tablespoons melted butter
235 ml/1 cup boiling water
2 baking sheets lined with baking parchment

MAKES ABOUT 15

Preheat the oven to 175°C (350°F) Gas 4.

Put the oats, peppercorns, salt and bicarbonate of soda/baking soda in a food processor and pulse to mix. Pour in the melted butter and boiling water and process until a dough begins to form.

Turn the dough onto a floured work surface. Roll out to a long rectangle 15 cm/6 inches wide, then cut into strips 2.5 cm/1 inch wide and lay on the prepared baking sheets.

Bake in the preheated oven for 15–18 minutes until golden brown, then cool on wire racks. Store in an airtight container at room temperature.

Eat this cheesy, peppery shortbread plain or top with a little dollop of salty tapenade. I mark them with a stamp that my sister Elvena gave to me, but you can use a fork.

Parmesan pepper shortbread

270 g/2 cups plain/all-purpose flour
80 g/1 cup finely grated Parmesan cheese
2 teaspoons coarsely ground Malabar peppercorns
1 tablespoon fresh thyme leaves
225 g/2 sticks salted butter, chilled and cubed
1 tablespoon coarse sea salt
2 baking sheets lined with baking parchment
a 6-cm/2½-inch round cookie cutter

MAKES ABOUT 27

Put the flour, Parmesan, pepper and thyme in a food processor and combine. Add the butter and process until the dough comes together.

Turn the dough out onto a floured work surface and knead for a few minutes, then roll out to a thickness of 5 mm/¼ inch. Cut out rounds using the cookie cutter and place on the prepared baking sheets. Gather up and re-roll the scraps until all the dough has been used. Mark the top of the biscuits with a fork or leave plain. Place the sheets in the freezer for 15 minutes to chill.

Preheat the oven to 175°C (350°F) Gas 4.

Remove the shortbread from the freezer. Sprinkle with salt and bake in the preheated oven for 12–15 minutes until golden brown. Remove and cool on a wire rack.

A taste of Greece in a pan, salty feta sprinkled with citrus pepper and wrapped up in a briny vine leaf makes a wonderful mezze dish for sharing.

Vine-wrapped feta parcels

450 g/1 lb. feta cheese

24 brined vine leaves

2 tablespoons ground Citrus Pepper peppermill mix (page 53)

peel of 1 lemon, cut into strips

olive oil, to cover

MAKES 24

Cut the feta into 24 cubes. Lay the vine leaves out on a worksurface and place a piece of feta at the stem end of each leaf. Sprinkle with the peppermill mix.

Fold the two sides of the leaf over the feta, then roll the leaf up like a cigar. Repeat to make 24 parcels. Place the feta parcels in a glass dish. Sprinkle with the lemon peel and pour olive oil over to cover.

Cover and refrigerate for at least 1 week before serving. The parcels will keep for up to 1 month in the fridge.

Jewelled bright green Italian Castelvetrano olives are perfect for pan frying. Mixed with citrus and salty capers, they are a taste of the Italian countryside.

Peppered pan-roasted olives

2 tablespoons olive oil

225 g/8 oz. unpitted Castelvetrano olives

2 slices of dried tangerine or orange

½ teaspoon crushed Smoked Pepper peppermill mix (page 53)

2 teaspoons salted capers

SERVES 4-6

Heat the oil in a frying pan/skillet over a medium heat. Add the olives, tangerine slices, peppermill mix and salted capers and fry for 3–4 minutes.

Tip into a bowl and serve immediately.

Main dishes

The thing I love most about pho is all the sauces and herbs that go along with it. You can make a simple bowl or go to town and really dress it up – there are no rules!

Peppered beef pho

1.5 litres/6 cups good-quality chicken stock
2 star anise
2.5-cm/1-inch piece of fresh ginger
2 tablespoons fish sauce
2 tablespoons toasted sesame oil
3 tablespoons soy sauce
1 tablespoon sambal oelek (Asian chilli/chile paste)
1 teaspoon Lampong peppercorns, cracked
1 garlic clove, finely chopped
450 g/1 lb. sirloin steak
600 g/4 cups cooked rice noodles
115 g/2 cups beansprouts
135 g/1 cup grated carrot
3 spring onions/scallions, finely sliced
2 red chillies/chiles, finely sliced
selection of fresh Vietnamese basil, mint, coriander/cilantro, lime wedges and chilli/chile sauce, to serve

SERVES 4

Pour the chicken stock into a saucepan and add the star anise, ginger and fish sauce. Bring to the boil, then reduce the heat and simmer for 20 minutes.

In a shallow bowl whisk together the sesame oil, soy sauce, sambal oelek, peppercorns and garlic. Add the steak and coat with the marinade.

Set a heavy-based cast-iron pan/skillet over a high heat until smoking. Add the steak and sear for 2 minutes on each side, then transfer to a cutting board. Reduce the heat and add the remainder of the marinade to the pan. Cook for a few minutes until thickened, then pour into a small bowl. Slice the steak into thin strips.

Divide the noodles, beansprouts and grated carrot into four large bowls. Top with strips of steak and pour over the hot broth. Sprinkle with the onions and chillies/chiles. Serve with the fresh herbs, lime wedges and sauce.

Drambuie hails from Scotland and is made from whisky infused with spices, heather honey and herbs. It is believed to be a recipe created for Bonnie Prince Charlie. Lacing it through a pepper sauce adds wonderful warmth, and it is especially good with steak.

Pepper-crusted steak *with Drambuie sauce*

680 g/1½ lb. Porterhouse or T-bone steak, 3.5 cm/1½ inches thick
1 tablespoon fresh thyme leaves, plus a few stalks to garnish
2 tablespoons olive oil
4 teaspoons cracked rainbow peppercorns
30 g/2 tablespoons salted butter
1 shallot, finely diced
1 garlic clove, finely chopped
120 ml/½ cup double/heavy cream
120 ml/½ cup beef stock
4 tablespoons Drambuie
sea salt, to taste

SERVES 2

Put the steak in a ceramic dish and season with salt. Mix together the thyme, half the olive oil and 3 teaspoons of the peppercorns and spread over the steak to make a crust.

Set a heavy-based cast-iron pan/skillet over a high heat until smoking, then add the steak. Cook for 8 minutes, then turn over, reduce the heat to medium and cook for a further 5 minutes. Transfer the steak to a warm plate, cover with foil and rest for 10 minutes.

Put the remaining olive oil in the pan along with the butter and stir to melt. Add the remaining peppercorns, shallot and garlic, and stir. Cook for 4–5 minutes over a medium heat until golden brown. Stir in the cream, stock and Drambuie and bring to the boil, then reduce the heat and simmer for a few minutes. Season with salt and pour into a small jug/pitcher.

Slice the steak, garnish with the thyme stalks and serve with the sauce.

I love making curries, partly due to all the beautifully coloured ingredients that go into them. This curry is laced with spicy and aromatic crushed Malabar peppercorns from India's south-west coast. Dried fruit adds a touch of sweetness to the dish.

Indian pepper chicken

8 chicken thighs, skin on, bone in

2 teaspoons ground Malabar peppercorns

1 teaspoon sea salt

4 tablespoons ghee or olive oil

1 large onion, diced

2 garlic cloves, finely chopped

1 teaspoon curry powder

1 teaspoon turmeric

1 teaspoon ancho chilli powder

1 teaspoon ground cumin

4 sprigs of fresh curry leaves

475 ml/2 cups chicken stock

70 g/½ cup (dark) raisins or dried dates

naan bread, to serve

SERVES 4

Sprinkle the chicken thighs with the pepper and salt, making sure they are completely coated.

Set a large frying pan/skillet over a medium–high heat and add 3 tablespoons of the ghee or oil. Put the chicken skin-side down in the pan and sauté for about 4 minutes, until golden brown. Turn the chicken over and brown the other side, then transfer to a large plate.

Add the remaining ghee or oil to the pan, and add the onion and garlic and cook until golden brown (about 5 minutes). Add the curry powder, turmeric, chilli powder and cumin, and stir to combine. Cook for 2 minutes.

Return the chicken to the pan, skin-side down, and top with the curry leaves. Pour over the chicken stock and bring to the boil, then reduce the heat to a simmer and cover the pan with a lid or foil. Cook for 30 minutes.

Remove the lid and toss in the raisins or dates. Turn the chicken thighs over and continue to cook uncovered for another 30 minutes.

Serve the chicken with the sauce and warm naan bread.

Roast chicken is one of my favourite dinners, and roasting it with a lovely layer of briny green peppercorn butter makes it even better. A play on the classic steak au poivre, it is delicious.

Chicken au poivre

60 g/4 tablespoons butter, at room
    temperature
2 tablespoons brined green
    peppercorns
grated zest of 1 lemon
2 tablespoons lemon juice
1 teaspoon sea salt, plus extra
    to season
1.8 kg/4 lbs. chicken
olive oil, to drizzle
1 head of garlic, cut in half
a few sprigs of fresh thyme
60 ml/¼ cup white wine

Sauce
1 tablespoon brined green
    peppercorns
1 shallot, sliced
200 ml/1 cup white wine
200 ml/1 cup double/heavy cream

SERVES 4

Preheat the oven to 190°C (375°F) Gas 5.

Put the butter, peppercorns, lemon zest and juice and salt in a food processor and process until combined.

Put the chicken in a roasting pan. Using a knife, make a pocket between the skin and the flesh on the chicken breast and stuff with the pepper butter. Smooth out with your hands, making sure the butter is evenly distributed. Rub any leftover butter over the top of the chicken, then drizzle with olive oil and sprinkle with sea salt.

Add the garlic and sprigs of thyme to the pan and pour in the wine. Roast in the oven for 1 hour, then remove from the oven. Spoon 4 tablespoons of the cooking juices into a frying pan/skillet for the sauce. Cover the chicken with foil and rest for 15 minutes.

To make the sauce, set the frying pan/skillet over a medium–high heat and add the peppercorns and shallot to the cooking juices. Take one of the roasted garlic halves and squeeze the garlic into the pan. Cook for 3 minutes, squashing the garlic down to a paste. Add the wine and cream and bring to a boil, then reduce the heat to a lively simmer. Season with salt and cook for 10 minutes, stirring occasionally. Pour into a jug/pitcher and serve alongside the chicken.

Pork belly is one of my all-time favourites. Slowly roast it to a dark, crispy crust and then top with sweet, juicy plums. In winter serve it with noodles or rice, and in summer keep it simple with a large, crisp green salad. Allow plenty of marinating time for the best flavour.

Szechuan roasted pork belly *with plums*

a 1.5-kg/3½-lb. piece of pork belly

2 teaspoons sea salt

70 g/¼ cup orange-blossom honey

60 ml/¼ cup soy sauce

60 ml/¼ cup rice wine vinegar

1 tablespoon toasted sesame oil

1 tablespoon sambal oelek (Asian chilli/chile paste)

1 tablespoon crushed Szechuan peppercorns

4 garlic cloves

a 5-cm/2-inch piece of fresh ginger, peeled

½ teaspoon ground cinnamon

6 medium plums, halved and pitted

SERVES 6

Put the pork belly on a work surface. Score the skin and rub all over with the salt.

Put the honey, soy sauce, vinegar, sesame oil, sambal oelek, peppercorns, garlic, ginger and cinnamon in a blender and process until smooth. Pour the mixture into a baking dish and lay the pork on top, skin side down. Spoon the mixture over the pork to coat evenly. Cover and refrigerate for 6–24 hours.

Remove the pork from the fridge, uncover and bring to room temperature.

Preheat the oven to 175°C (350°F) Gas 4.

Place the pork in the oven and roast for 2 hours, basting every 30 minutes.

Remove the pork from the oven and drain off the excess fat. Turn the pork skin side up in the pan so that it crisps. Arrange the plums around the pork and return to the oven for 30–40 minutes. Remove from the oven and tent with foil. Rest for 15 minutes.

To serve, cut into thick slices and top with the roasted plums.

Gochujang is a red pepper paste used in Korean cooking. It comes in varying degrees of heat, so make sure to check the label and choose something to suit your tastebuds. These ribs are great for the barbecue; serve them with an Asian coleslaw or kimchi.

Korean sticky ribs

8 Korean-style beef ribs, 1 cm/½ inch thick
3 spring onions/scallions, finely sliced
2 tablespoons black sesame seeds

Marinade
60 ml/¼ cup soy sauce
60 ml/¼ cup toasted sesame oil
140 g/½ cup orange-blossom honey
2 heaped tablespoons gochujang
1 tablespoon fish sauce
4 garlic cloves, bashed
2 Serrano chillies/chiles, chopped
2 teaspoons cracked rainbow peppercorns
½ teaspoon sea salt

Pickled carrots & raisins (optional)
6 carrots, grated
100 g/¾ cup raisins
2 shallots, thinly sliced
1 teaspoon Lampong peppercorns, coarsely chopped
1 quantity of Basic Pickle Mix (page 54)
½ teaspoon ground cumin
½ teaspoon ground coriander

SERVES 4

Lay the ribs in a single layer in a ceramic baking dish.

Put all the marinade ingredients in a blender and process until smooth. Pour over the ribs and sprinkle with the spring onions/scallions and sesame seeds. Cover and refrigerate for 6–24 hours.

Remove the ribs from the fridge and bring to room temperature.

Heat a grill/broiler or barbecue to a medium–high heat. Place the ribs on the rack and cook for 5 minutes, then turn over and cook for another 5 minutes. Transfer to a warm plate and tent with foil. Rest for 10 minutes.

Put the remaining marinade in a small saucepan and bring to the boil, then reduce the heat and simmer for 5 minutes. To serve, pour the marinade into a bowl and serve alongside the ribs and pickled carrots and raisins, if desired.

Pickled carrots & raisins *(pictured page 55)*

The pickled carrots and raisins need to be made at least 1 week in advance to allow the flavours to infuse. Layer the carrot, raisins, shallots and peppercorns in a sterilized jar. Bring the Basic Pickle Mix to the boil, then add the cumin and coriander, and stir to dissolve the sugar. Cook for 3 minutes, then pour into the jar and screw the lid on. Seal following the instructions on page 54.

Delicately perfumed with kaffir lime leaves and lemongrass, this curry is given a little kick with the addition of green peppercorns and fresh chillies/chiles. Serve it up with lots of fragrant herbs and juicy limes to squeeze.

Green coconut shrimp curry

2 tablespoons coconut oil
820 ml/3½ cups coconut milk
45 g/1 cup dried unsweetened
   coconut flakes
450 g/1 lb. prawns/shrimp, peeled,
   tails on
fresh coriander/cilantro, to serve
kaffir or regular limes, to serve

Curry paste
2 Serrano chillies, roughly chopped
a 5-cm/2-inch piece of fresh ginger,
   peeled and sliced
3 stalks of lemongrass, white part
   only, sliced
3 garlic cloves
2 teaspoons green peppercorns
2 teaspoons shrimp paste
1 teaspoon ground coriander
6 kaffir lime leaves
grated zest and juice of 1 kaffir
   or regular lime
2 tablespoons fish sauce

SERVES 4

Put all the ingredients for the curry paste in a blender or food processer and process until they form a paste.

Set a deep frying pan/skillet over a medium–high heat and add the coconut oil. Add the curry paste and cook for 3–4 minutes, stirring continuously. Add the coconut milk and flakes to the pan and stir to combine. Bring to the boil, then reduce the heat and simmer for 20 minutes.

Increase the heat and bring the mixture back to the boil. Add the prawns/shrimp, cover and cook for 5–6 minutes until they are pink and cooked through.

Remove from the heat and rest for 5 minutes. Spoon into bowls and sprinkle with coriander/cilantro leaves. Serve with limes to squeeze.

I grew up in Scotland catching mackerel off our boat, so I have a fondness for these delicious oily fish. Escabeche is a preserving technique that is widely used throughout the Mediterranean. I like making this for a weekend lunch, as it's a prepare-ahead, no-stress recipe that allows you to spend time with your friends instead of being stuck in the kitchen.

Mackerel escabeche *with pickles*

4 mackerel fillets, boned, skin on

2 tablespoons extra virgin olive oil

4 shallots, finely sliced

1 carrot, grated

2 teaspoons Tellicherry peppercorns

3 garlic cloves, finely sliced

2 bay leaves

2 teaspoons Piment d'Espelette
  or chilli/hot red pepper flakes

350 ml/1½ cups white wine

235 ml/1 cup white wine vinegar

sea salt and freshly ground black
  pepper, to taste

crusty bread, to serve

Curried cauliflower

150 g/2 cups cauliflower florets

1 large fennel, thinly sliced

1 quantity of Basic Pickle Mix (page 54)

1 teaspoon curry powder

1 teaspoon mustard seeds

1 teaspoon white peppercorns

SERVES 4

You need to make the curried cauliflower at least 1 week in advance to allow the flavours to infuse. Layer the vegetables in a sterilized jar. Bring the Basic Pickle Mix to the boil, stirring to dissolve the sugar, then stir in the curry powder, mustard seeds and peppercorns. Cook for 3 minutes, then pour into the jar and screw the lid on. Seal following the instructions on page 54.

Season the mackerel with salt and pepper, and set aside.

Pour the olive oil into a medium pan over a low heat. Add the shallots, carrot, peppercorns, garlic, bay leaves and d'Espelette or chilli/hot red pepper flakes. Stir to combine and continue to cook for 3–4 minutes over a low heat, allowing the vegetables to sweat.

Increase the heat, then add the wine and vinegar, and season with a pinch of salt. Bring to the boil, then reduce to a simmer for 20 minutes.

Arrange the mackerel in the pan and spoon over some of the vegetables and juices. Cook for 3 minutes, then remove from the heat. Cover with a lid and cool. Place the pan in the fridge for 4–24 hours.

When ready to serve, place a fillet on each plate with a little of the juices and serve with the pickled cauliflower and some crusty bread.

Buy sushi-grade ahi (or yellowfin) tuna to make this dish and wrap it up in a citrusy pepper crust. The lemony yuzu juice is a must, but if you can't find it you can use lemon juice. Shiso is a wonderful citrus-flavoured herb, but you could use other leaves, such as basil.

Citrus ahi tuna *with yuzu dipping sauce*

450 g/1 lb. sushi-grade ahi (or yellowfin) tuna
2 teaspoons finely chopped dried orange peel
4 teaspoons ground green peppercorns
1 teaspoon sea salt
2 tablespoons sunflower oil
shiso leaves, to serve, optional

Dipping sauce
1 tablespoon yuzu juice
2 teaspoons sesame oil
1 tablespoon soy sauce
1 teaspoon grated fresh ginger
1 teaspoon finely chopped green chilli/chile
a pinch of brown sugar

SERVES 2

To make the dipping sauce, whisk all the ingredients together. Pour into a bowl and set aside.

Rinse the tuna under cold running water and pat dry. Cut the tuna into two rectangles and set aside.

Mix the orange peel, peppercorns and salt together on a large plate, then roll the tuna in the mix to completely cover.

Set a large frying pan/skillet over a medium–high heat and pour in the oil. When the pan is smoking, add the tuna and sear on all sides for about 3 minutes in total. You want the middle of the tuna to remain raw.

Transfer the tuna from the pan to a cutting board and rest for a few minutes. Place a few shiso leaves on two plates. Cut the tuna into slices 2.5 cm/1 inch thick and arrange on the leaves. Serve with the dipping sauce.

This recipe, using spicy, citrusy Sansho pepper, is my spin on the ever-popular salt and pepper prawns/shrimp served in Chinese restaurants around the world. Dip the freshly fried squid into the spiced mayo and enjoy.

Salt and pepper squid *with Sansho spicy dip*

½ teaspoon ground Sansho pepper
2 teaspoons sea salt
65 g/½ cup rice flour
450 g/1 lb. squid, cleaned and sliced
freshly squeezed juice of 1 lemon
vegetable oil, for frying

Dip
115 g/½ cup good-quality mayonnaise
5 g/¼ cup Vietnamese or regular basil
   leaves
½ teaspoon Sansho pepper
½ teaspoon sea salt
grated zest of 1 lemon

SERVES 4

To make the dip, whisk all the ingredients together in a small bowl until well combined. Set aside.

In a large shallow bowl mix together the Sansho pepper, salt and rice flour. Put the squid in another bowl and pour over the lemon juice.

Pour enough oil to come halfway up a large saucepan, then place over a medium–high heat until the oil starts to simmer.

Take a few pieces of squid at a time and toss in the flour mixture to coat. Working in batches, deep fry for 2–3 minutes until golden and cooked through. Transfer to a wire rack to drain.

Pile the cooked squid in a shallow bowl and serve with the dip.

I love the slight sweetness of the maple syrup combined with the earthiness of the spice, then topped with a breath of the ocean with nori seaweed. Serve the tofu warm or chilled – either way it's heaven in a bowl.

Spicy maple baked tofu *with buckwheat noodles*

450 g/1 lb. firm organic tofu
70 ml/⅓ cup good-quality maple syrup
1 tablespoon olive oil
2 teaspoons smoked pimentón
1 teaspoon freshly cracked Tellicherry pepper
a pinch of sea salt
270 g/9½ oz. buckwheat soba noodles
tamari or soy sauce, to drizzle
1 sheet of nori seaweed, crumbled or finely sliced

SERVES 4

Preheat the oven to 200°C (400°F) Gas 6.

Slice the tofu into pieces 1 cm/½ inch thick and arrange in a single layer in a ceramic baking dish.

In a medium bowl whisk together the maple syrup, olive oil, smoked pimentón, pepper and sea salt. Pour over the tofu to coat, then bake in the preheated oven for 30 minutes.

Bring a large pan of water to boil over a high heat and add the noodles. Cook for 4 minutes, then drain, rinse under cold water and set aside.

To serve, divide the noodles between four bowls and drizzle with a touch of tamari or soy sauce. Top with a couple of pieces of tofu and sprinkle with a little of the seaweed.

A wonderful artisanal gnocchi that you will make over and over again. The flavours are gentle and fresh with a little kick from the pepper. Dusted in lashings of Parmesan and drizzled with good olive oil and fresh lemon, it is a perfect dish all year round, as a simple spring supper or a hearty dinner served alongside short ribs or stews.

Lemon pepper ricotta gnocchi

450 g/2 cups Homemade Ricotta (page 12)

grated zest of 2 large lemons

20 g/¼ cup freshly grated Parmesan cheese, plus extra to serve

100 g/¾ cup plain/all-purpose flour, plus extra for dusting

1 large egg, beaten

½ teaspoon ground white pepper, plus extra for dusting

½ teaspoon sea salt

extra virgin olive oil

20 g/½ cup torn mixed fresh herbs of your choice

SERVES 4–6

In a large bowl mix the ricotta, half the lemon zest, Parmesan, flour, egg, pepper and salt until well combined.

Turn out onto a work surface lightly dusted with flour and roll into a ball. Divide into four pieces. Taking one piece at a time, roll into a thin sausage shape. Repeat with the other pieces. Using a sharp knife, cut the dough into pieces 2.5 cm/1 inch long.

Bring a large pasta pot of salted water to the boil. Add the gnocchi and cook for a few minutes. They will float to the surface when cooked.

Drain and toss into a large bowl. Drizzle liberally with olive oil and add the remaining lemon zest, extra Parmesan and the herbs. Toss and serve in bowls with a dusting of white pepper to finish.

Sweet things

In summer, when strawberry season arrives, it's the time to make these divine little shortcakes. With lashings of thick mascarpone tucked in between, this is a dessert to remember.

Summer shortcake *with peppered strawberries*

280 g/2 cups sliced strawberries

225 g/1 cup mascarpone

Shortbread

200 g/1½ cups plain/all-purpose flour,
　plus extra for dusting

2 teaspoons baking powder

3 tablespoons demerara or turbinado
　sugar, plus extra for sprinkling

60 g/4 tablespoons cold butter,
　cut into small pieces

½ teaspoon sea salt

190 ml/⅔ cup plus 2 tablespoons
　double/heavy cream, cold

Syrup

200 g/1 cup white sugar

1 teaspoon freshly cracked black
　Malabar peppercorns

a 7.5-cm/3-inch round cookie cutter

a baking sheet lined with baking
　parchment

SERVES 6

Preheat the oven to 190°C (375°F) Gas 5.

Put the flour, baking powder, demerara or turbinado sugar, butter and salt in a food processor and pulse until the mixture resembles large breadcrumbs. Pour in the cream and continue to pulse until the mixture just comes together.

Turn the dough out on to a lightly floured work surface and roll out to a thickness of 2.5 cm/1 inch. Using the cookie cutter, cut out 6 circles. Arrange the shortcakes on the prepared baking sheet 2.5 cm/1 inch apart and sprinkle with sugar. Bake in the preheated oven for 20 minutes.

To make the syrup, place the sugar and peppercorns in a small pan with 120 ml/½ cup water over a medium–high heat. Bring to a boil, stirring occasionally, until the sugar has dissolved. Reduce to a simmer and cook for 10 minutes, then remove from the heat and strain into a bowl. Add the strawberries and cool.

To serve, split the shortcakes in half. Generously spread the bottom halves with mascarpone and spoon the strawberries and syrup on top. Place the shortcake tops on and serve.

Delicate goat's cheese panna cotta topped with sweet, heady candied cherries will make your guests very happy. If you can't find goat's milk yogurt, then just use regular full-fat yogurt. In winter I top it with peppery candied blood oranges.

Goat's cheese panna cotta *with candied peppered cherries*

Panna cotta
2 teaspoons gelatin
475 ml/2 cups double/heavy cream
100 g/½ cup white sugar
115 g/4 oz. soft goat's cheese, at room
    temperature
215 g/1 cup goat's milk yogurt

Candied peppered cherries
100 g/½ cup white sugar
1 teaspoon crushed pink peppercorns
300 g/2 cups pitted cherries, halved

SERVES 6

Dissolve the gelatin in 2 tablespoons of warm water and set aside.

Bring the cream and sugar to the boil in a pan over a medium–high heat, stirring constantly. Reduce the heat to a simmer and continue to cook for 5 minutes, until the sugar has completely dissolved. Remove from the heat and whisk in the goat's cheese, yogurt and gelatin until smooth.

Pour into six ramekins and set aside to cool, then cover and refrigerate for 4–24 hours.

To make the syrup for the cherries, place the sugar and peppercorns in a small pan with 60 ml/¼ cup of water over medium–high heat. Bring to the boil, stirring occasionally, until the sugar has dissolved, then reduce the heat to a simmer and cook for 10 minutes. Remove from the heat, add the cherries and set aside to cool.

To serve, spoon the cooled candied peppered cherries and their syrup on top of the panna cotta.

Delightful little pots packed with spicy, boozy flavours. I like to make these for casual outside dinners in the summer. They are a breeze to whip up and are also great for picnics – I pour the mousse into easily transportable individual jars with lids.

Pepper bourbon chocolate pots

140 ml/⅔ cup double/heavy cream
2 teaspoons instant espresso powder
2 teaspoons Lampong peppercorns, coarsely chopped
1 tablespoon bourbon or whiskey
300 g/10½ oz. dark/bittersweet chocolate (72% cocoa solids)
6 egg whites
2 tablespoons caster/superfine sugar
crème fraîche, to serve
edible flowers, to garnish (optional)

SERVES 6

Pour the cream into a small pan and add the espresso powder and peppercorns. Bring to the boil, stirring constantly, then remove from the heat and cool. Strain through a fine sieve into a small bowl, then stir in the bourbon or whiskey.

Melt the chocolate over a medium heat in a double boiler, or in a heatproof bowl set over a pan of simmering water. Remove from the heat and stir in the espresso pepper cream to combine. Set aside.

In a large bowl whisk the egg whites with an electric beater until stiff peaks form, then add the sugar and whisk to combine.

Add the chocolate mixture to the egg whites a spoonful at a time and gently fold together. Divide the mixture between six small bowls or pots. Refrigerate for 4–24 hours.

To serve, add a dollop of crème fraîche to the top of each chocolate pot. If you wish, garnish with edible flowers.

Wonderful spicy chilli powder, pepper and smoked paprika spike against the almonds and sweetness of the praline. If you wish, you can omit the chocolate swirled on top. Fun to serve at a dinner party as one big dramatic sheet for guests to break, or crush up and serve sprinkled on top of ice cream.

Mexican praline

200 g/1½ cups raw almonds,
  coarsely chopped
2 teaspoons ancho chilli powder
2 teaspoons cracked rainbow
  peppercorns
½ teaspoon smoked paprika
600 g/3 cups white sugar
100g/3½ oz. dark/bittersweet
  chocolate, 72% cocoa solids
a large baking sheet, lightly oiled

**MAKES ENOUGH TO GARNISH
6 DESSERTS**

Put the almonds, chilli powder, peppercorns and smoked paprika in a saucepan over a medium–high heat and toast for 2–3 minutes. Tip out onto the prepared baking sheet and spread evenly.

Pour the sugar into a medium saucepan, add 150 ml/⅔ cup water and bring to the boil over medium–high heat. Boil the syrup undisturbed for approximately 8–10 minutes until it is a dark golden brown and the sugar has dissolved. You can swirl the pan as the syrup darkens. Pour evenly over the almond mixture and allow to set.

Melt the chocolate over a medium heat in a double boiler, or in a heatproof bowl set over a pan of simmering water. Using a fork, drizzle the melted chocolate over the praline and allow to set.

Store in an airtight container for up to 1 week.

Very popular at Christmas time, these German cookies are filled with spices and pepper. You can dust them lightly with peppered sugar or completely coat them to make them festive. If there should be any left over, they make a lovely addition to a trifle.

Pfeffernüsse cookies

300 g/2¼ cups plain/all-purpose flour
1 teaspoon ground ginger
½ teaspoon ground cinnamon
½ teaspoon ground allspice
¼ teaspoon ground nutmeg
¼ teaspoon bicarbonate of soda/
   baking soda
2 teaspoons finely ground white
   pepper
115 g/1 stick butter, at room
   temperature
150 g/¾ cup soft dark brown sugar
85 g/¼ cup molasses or dark treacle
1 medium egg
70 g/½ cup icing/confectioner's sugar
*2 baking sheets lined with baking
   parchment*

MAKES ABOUT 36

Sift the flour, ginger, cinnamon, allspice, nutmeg, bicarbonate of soda/baking soda and half the pepper into a bowl.

Put the butter, sugar and molasses in the bowl of an electric mixer and beat for about 5 minutes until fluffy. Add the egg and continue to beat until fully combined. Reduce the speed and slowly beat in the flour mixture.

Scoop out 1 tablespoon of dough at a time and roll into balls. Place on the prepared baking sheets 5 cm/2 inches apart. Put in the freezer for 15 minutes.

Preheat the oven to 175°C (350°F) Gas 4.

Remove the cookies from the freezer and bake in the preheated oven for 15 minutes until golden brown. Transfer to wire racks to cool.

In a small bowl, mix together the icing/confectioner's sugar and remaining pepper. When the cookies have completely cooled, sprinkle with the sugar mix. Store in an airtight container for up to 2 weeks.

Preserves,
mustards & oils

Use these mixes to flavour stews, pasta dishes and stir fries, to infuse oils and pickles, or mix into oil to make a wet rub or marinade.

Each mix uses the same method. Mix all the ingredients together and store in a glass jar with a tight fitting lid. To use, spoon the mix into a peppermill.

Peppermill mixes

Moroccan rose petal

1½ heaped teaspoons Tellicherry
  peppercorns
1½ teaspoons caraway seeds
½ teaspoon ground cardamom
1½ teaspoons dried chilli/hot red
  pepper flakes
2 long peppercorns (*Piper longum*)
½ cinnamon stick, crushed
60 g/½ cup edible dried organic rose
  petals
1 teaspoon pink peppercorns

Dried hibiscus

45 g/⅓ cup edible dried organic
  hibiscus flowers, crushed
1 tablespoon pink peppercorns
2 long peppercorns (*Piper longum*)

Citrus pepper

3 tablespoons white peppercorns
1 tablespoon dried lemon peel
1 tablespoon dried orange peel

Chinese Five-spice pepper

2 tablespoons Szechuan peppercorns
1 cinnamon stick, crushed
2 teaspoons allspice berries, crushed
1 teaspoon whole cloves
1 teaspoon ground ginger
1 teaspoon fennel seeds

Hachimi Togarashi

2 teaspoons Sansho peppercorns
1 sheet of nori seaweed, crumbled
  (about 2 tablespoons)
2 teaspoons black sesame seeds
2 teaspoons dried orange peel
1 teaspoons dried chilli/hot red
  pepper flakes
1 teaspoon chilli powder
½ teaspoon ground ginger
½ teaspoon garlic powder

Smoked pepper

2 tablespoons smoked black
  peppercorns
1 tablespoon dried chilli/hot red
  pepper flakes
1 teaspoon coarse garlic powder
1 teaspoon fenugreek seeds
2 teaspoons smoked paprika
1 dried bay leaf, crumbled

Berbere pepper

2 tablespoons Malabar peppercorns
1 tablespoon ground hot paprika
1 teaspoon ground paprika
1 teaspoon ground cardamom
1 teaspoon ground ginger
1 cinnamon stick, crushed
1 teaspoon allspice berries
1 teaspoon coarse garlic powder
½ teaspoon fenugreek seeds

Clockwise from top left: Hachimi Togarashi, Chinese Five-spice pepper, Moroccan rose petal, Dried hibiscus, Smoked pepper, Berbere pepper, Citrus pepper

Pickles are wonderfully fresh and crunchy. Each recipe makes about 500 g/ 2 cups. To seal, screw the lid on the jar while still warm, turn it upside down to cool completely, then put in the refrigerator for at least 1 week before eating or storing in the cupboard. Once opened, consume within 6 months.

Pepper pickles

Basic pickle mix

475 ml/2 cups white wine vinegar
100 g/½ cup sugar
1 teaspoon coarse sea salt
1 bay leaf

Watermelon rind

2.25 kg/5 lb. mini watermelon
3 tablespoons coarse sea salt
475 ml/2 cups white wine vinegar
200 g/1 cup white sugar
1 tablespoon rainbow peppercorns
2 teaspoons Piment d'Espelette or chilli/hot red pepper flakes

Cut the watermelon into wedges and scoop the flesh out, leaving 1 cm/½ inch of flesh attached to the rind, then cut into small cubes.

Pour 1.4 litres/6 cups water into a saucepan, add the salt and bring to the boil. Add the watermelon rind and boil for 5 minutes, then drain and pour into a large jar.

In a pan bring the vinegar to the boil with the sugar, peppercorns and d'Espelette or chilli/hot red pepper flakes, stirring to dissolve the sugar. Cook for 5 minutes, then pour over the fruit and seal as above.

Peppery cucumbers

6 Persian cucumbers, thinly sliced
1 quantity of Basic Pickle Mix
1½ teaspoons Szechuan peppercorns

Layer the cucmbers in a sterilized jar. Bring the Basic Pickle Mix and the peppercorns to the boil, stirring to dissolve the sugar. Cook for 3 minutes, then pour into the jar and seal as above.

Spicy kumquats

24 kumquats, halved
3 jalapeños, thinly sliced
1 cinnamon stick
2 star anise
2 teaspoons Malabar peppercorns
1 quantity of Basic Pickle Mix

Layer all the ingredients except for the Basic Pickle Mix in a sterilized jar. Bring the Basic Pickle Mix to the boil, stirring to dissolve the sugar, and cook for 3 minutes, then pour into the jar and seal as above.

Japanese radishes

4 watermelon (or 6 regular) radishes
12 shishito (or Padrón) peppers, sliced
3 jalapeños, thinly sliced
1½ teaspoons Sansho pepper
1 quantity of Basic Pickle Mix
¼ cup sake (rice wine)

Layer all the ingredients except for the Basic Pickle Mix and sake in a sterilized jar. Bring the Basic Pickle Mix and sake to the boil, stirring to dissolve the sugar. Cook for 3 minutes, then pour into the jar and seal as above.

Clockwise from top left: Peppery cucumbers, Watermelon rind, Carrots & raisins (page 28), Chai apples (page 61), Spicy kumquats, Curried cauliflower (page 32), Japanese radishes

In summer at the height of peach season, make a batch of this delicious chutney. The punch comes from the black Kerala peppercorns that impart a wonderfully bold flavour.

Peppered peach chutney

12 firm ripe peaches, halved and pitted
4 yellow onions, roughly chopped
5 garlic cloves, finely chopped
2 teaspoons each of ground cumin, ground coriander, chilli powder, whole Kerala peppercorns and curry powder
1 teaspoon mustard seeds
2 cinnamon sticks
3 bay leaves
355 ml/1½ cups apple cider vinegar
450 g/2¼ cups demerara or turbinado sugar

**MAKES ABOUT
1.15 LITRES/5 CUPS**

Preheat the oven to 200°C (400°F) Gas 6.

Cut the peaches into 5-cm/2-inch pieces and put in a ceramic baking dish. Add the remaining ingredients apart from the sugar, and toss to combine. Bake in the preheated oven for 40 minutes, stirring halfway through. Add the sugar and stir. Return to the oven for another 55 minutes. Check every 15 minutes and stir to prevent burning.

Remove from the oven and allow it to sit for 5 minutes, then spoon into sterilized jars, leaving a 5-mm/¼-inch space at the top. Screw on the lids. Cool, then store in the fridge for 7–10 days before eating. Once open, store in the fridge for up to 3 months.

Dollop this spicy, smoky jam on top of a burger or serve alongside anything that comes off a fiery hot barbecue in the heat of the summer. It also makes a perfect partner to a cheeseboard for a casual get-together.

Tomato & smoked pepper jam

1.8 kg/4 lbs. tomatoes
2 tablespoons extra virgin olive oil
1 teaspoon sea salt
400 g/2 cups dark brown sugar
1 tablespoon harissa
1 tablespoon cracked smoked black peppercorns
1 cinnamon stick
2 tablespoons freshly squeezed lemon juice

**MAKES ABOUT
700 ML/3 CUPS**

Preheat the oven to 200°C (400°F) Gas 6.

Spread the tomatoes evenly on a baking sheet. Pour over the olive oil and sprinkle with the salt. Roast in the oven for 40 minutes until the skins have burst and are just slightly charred.

Put in a food processer and pulse until coarsely chopped, then tip into a medium-sized pan and add the sugar, harissa, peppercorns and cinnamon stick. Bring to the boil over a medium-high heat, stirring continuously. Reduce the heat to a simmer and cook for 40 minutes, stirring occasionally until the mixture becomes dark and thickens. Add the lemon juice and cook for a further 5 minutes.

Pour the jam into sterilized jars and screw the lids on. When cool, store in the fridge for up to 1 month.

Mustards are quick and easy to make. Use the same method for each of the mustards.

Mustards

Green peppercorn

75 g/½ cup yellow mustard seeds

175 ml/¾ cup cider vinegar

2 tablespoons cracked green peppercorns

2 tablespoons dark brown sugar

1 teaspoon freshly squeezed lemon juice

1 teaspoon sea salt

Smoked pepper

75 g/½ cup yellow mustard seeds

175 ml/¾ cup cider vinegar

1 tablespoon cracked smoked black peppercorns

1 tablespoon harissa

½ teaspoon ancho chilli powder

2 tablespoons dark brown sugar

1 teaspoon freshly squeezed lemon juice

1 teaspoon sea salt

Port & black pepper

75 g/½ cup yellow mustard seeds

120 ml/½ cup red wine vinegar

60 ml/¼ cup port

2 tablespoons cracked Tellicherry black peppercorns

2 tablespoons dark brown sugar

1 teaspoon sea salt

EACH MAKES 250 G/1 CUP

Dry-roast the mustard seeds in a hot pan for 2 minutes, then tip into a bowl and add the vinegar. Leave to soak overnight. Pour the mustard seeds and all the remaining ingredients into a blender. Process, adding a little more vinegar if the mixture is too stiff. Pour into sterilized jars, screw the lids on and refrigerate for up to 2 months.

Choose different kinds of oils, herbs, spices, nuts and fruits to make small batches of infused oils using the same method for each recipe.

Infused oils

Szechuan chilli/chile

235 ml/1 cup sunflower oil

2 tablespoons Szechuan peppercorns

Pepper Madras

235 ml/1 cup sunflower oil

1½ tablespoons long peppercorns

2 teaspoons Madras curry powder

Pepper ginger

235 ml/1 cup sunflower oil

50 g/⅓ cup crystallized ginger

1 tablespoon Malabar peppercorns

Rainbow rosemary

235 ml/1 cup olive oil

2 tablespoons rainbow peppercorns

2 sprigs of rosemary

EACH MAKES 250 G/1

Pour the oil into a small saucepan and bring to a simmer. Turn off the heat and add the remaining ingredients. Cool overnight. Next day, strain through a coffee filter into a sterilized glass jar with a lid (you can also leave it unstrained if you prefer). Store in the fridge for up to 1 month.

Clockwise from top left: Szechuan chilli/chile oil, Rainbow rosemary oil, Pepper Madras oil, Port & black pepper mustard, Smoked pepper mustard, Green peppercorn mustard, Pepper ginger oil

Drinks

Chai tea is one of those wonderful drinks that everyone has their own recipe for and there can be long, dizzying conversations debating it, especially while sipping it. Drink it hot or cold, and add a few little extras to make it your own.

Chai tea

1 teaspoon ground ginger
4–6 cardamom pods, bruised
1 cinnamon stick
2 star anise
1 teaspoon Tellicherry peppercorns
½ teaspoon whole cloves
2 teaspoons black tea
milk, to taste

SERVES 1

Put all the ingredients apart from the tea and milk in a pan along with 235 ml/1 cup water. Bring to the boil and cook for 2 minutes. Remove from the heat, add the tea and allow to steep for 5 minutes.

Strain into a cup or glass and add milk as desired. Add ice for a chilled version.

Chai apples *(pictured page 55)*

Layer 4 apples, cored and thinly sliced, with 150 g/1 cup of dried cranberries and 1 tablespoon of green peppercorns in a sterilized jar. Bring the Basic Pickle Mix (page 54) to the boil, adding 1 teaspoon of ground mixed chai spices used above (or a packet mix) and stirring to dissolve the sugar. Cook for 3 minutes, then pour into the jar and screw the lid on. Seal following the instructions on page 54 .

Boba (bubble tea) is a sweet Taiwanese drink made with large tapioca pearls. They come in a kaleidoscope of colours and flavours. This is to be sipped slowly on a hot day, without getting the pearls stuck in your straw! Wide straws are best.

Mango pepper boba

100 g/½ cup white sugar
6 kaffir lime leaves
340 g/2 cups chopped mango, fresh or frozen
350 g/2 cups ice
1 teaspoon Lampong peppercorns
75 g/1 cup cooked boba pearls (large tapioca balls)

SERVES 4

To make a simple syrup, put the sugar in a pan with 60 ml/¼ cup water over a medium heat and simmer until the sugar has dissolved. Add the lime leaves, then remove from the heat and set aside to cool.

Place the cooled simple syrup, mango, ice and peppercorns in a blender and process until smooth. Divide the pearls between the glasses, then top with the mango juice. Add a wide straw to each drink and serve.

This is a great way to infuse vodka. You can mix and match with other peppercorns, citrus and chillies/chiles. I like to use a Meyer lemon, as they have a wonderful perfume and aroma. Store in the freezer for an icy evening cocktail.

Pepper & lemon-infused vodka

1 Meyer lemon
70 cl–1 litre/24–34 fl oz. bottle of good-quality vodka

2 strings of brined green peppercorns

MAKES 1 BOTTLE

Cut the lemon into thin slices. Start layering by dropping a few pieces of lemon into the vodka bottle (or use a sterilized, wide-necked bottle) and add a string of peppercorns. Repeat, ending with a layer of lemon.

Seal and shake the bottle, then store in dark cool place for 1 month. Thereafter, store in the freezer until ready to use so it is kept ice cold.

When the sun is low in the sky and it's cocktail hour, the Lemon Drop is always welcome. Understated in its simplicity, it has a kick from the tart lemons and spicy infused peppercorn vodka. Sit back and sip slowly.

Peppered lemon drop

2 teaspoons crushed green peppercorns
1 teaspoon sugar
crushed ice
55 ml/2 fl. oz. Pepper & Lemon-infused Vodka (left)

30 ml/2 tablespoons simple syrup (see Mango Pepper Boba, page 61)
30 ml/2 tablespoons freshly squeezed lemon juice

SERVES 1

Mix together the crushed peppercorns and sugar on a small plate. Wet the rim of the glass and dip it into the pepper sugar and set aside.

Fill a cocktail shaker with crushed ice and pour in the vodka, simple syrup and lemon juice. Shake vigorously and pour into the prepared glass.

Index

Acknowledgments

Summer came and we once again gathered in my kitchen to cook and shoot with an array of wonderful peppercorns. Thank you to my dear friend Erin Kunkel for making the food sing with her beautiful photography. Alyse Sakai for assisting and all her hard work in the kitchen. Thank you to Julia Charles, Leslie Harrington, Stephanie Milner and Megan Smith for making this book happen. I no longer look at or think about peppercorns in the same way!